The Wine Lodge

Bernard Hagon

Introduction

The author, Bernard Hagon, with some of the regulars at Marsden's Wine Lodge, Islington, On the right is Bernard Willder, the author's best friend since his schooldays in Leigh on Sea.

This book is about the characters that came into Marsden's Wine Lodge. The story is true and not fiction. I hope you all enjoy the story about these lovely characters. I have used a few cockney slang words; I hope you will understand them.

My name is Bernard Hagon, and along with my wife, Jean Hagon, we took over the management of this 'Win Log' and purchased the premises a few years later. Some of the names in my story are fictitious, but others are true. I would like to dedicate this book to one of our customers: her name was "Lucienne" and she was 89 years of age. A beautiful old French lady and a lovely character whom we all adored. Her picture is on the front cover. We named her "The French cat with the hat".

One of my customers, who became a very good friend, was dying of cancer and only had a few weeks to live. Four years ago, he asked me to go and visit him in London for the last time. I had sold the wine lodge thirty-eight years earlier. I booked into the local Travelodge for two days and spent this time with him. He told me of the things he had done in his life, mostly robberies. He told me in detail of all that had happened on these occasions. I don't know whether it was a kind of confession to get it off his chest or not, but he told me everything, chapter and verse. He passed away three days later. I will tell you all about it in this book.

When I sold the wine bar and moved to Norfolk, we did not see each other for quite some time. however, he did visit us on one occasion many years ago. But he always kept in touch by phone and would ring us now and again. But he never revealed his telephone number. We really did take a liking to him, Jean and I, like so many of our customers that have kept in touch over the years. We retired over forty years ago. What Michael told me, I do not condone. I have been a law-abiding citizen all my life. However, there is an interesting story to be told. The wine bar, Marsden's Wine Lodge was in Upper Street, Islington. In 1977, the wine lodge was 390 years old – the oldest one in Great Britain under royal charter from Queen Anne, and registered with a City of London livery company. It had been neglected over many years by the accountants, who had run the establishment, not the owner, Colonel P C M Hingston. It was dirty and really rundown with just three or four customers per day. But to Jean and I this was great because there was only one way to go – and that was up.

Let me put you roughly into my background and Jean's. We had each come from a broken marriage and fell in love with each other when I had a public house in Essex. We decided to run away with each other and rented a bungalow in Watchet, Somerset, a very beautiful seaside fishing village where we stayed for a few months. After returning to London to stay with my mother in Bermondsey, I started to look for a job and found two advertisements in the newspapers. One was for a barman at the Savoy Hotel in central London, which I quite fancied; the other was for a wine bar manager in Upper Street, Islington, opposite the Town Hall.

I was given an appointment at the Savoy Hotel at eleven o'clock in the morning. To be honest, I was quite excited as it was a very prestigious place to work. The job on offer was cocktail bar manager. On arriving, I met up with the concierge who escorted me to Human Resources, where I met one of the managers and two HR colleagues. Extremely nice people. At the end of the interview, they said: 'You have been successful in your application, Mr Hagon. We will go through the relevant details on your arrival on Monday morning at nine o'clock.' Needless to say, I was extremely delighted at obtaining such a nice position at one of the country's top hotels.

At three o'clock on the same day, Jean and I had an appointment at the wine lodge in Islington with the accountants who run the establishment. Two gentlemen of Irish descent, both extremely pleasant, who made us feel very comfortable during their questioning procedure. After hearing about our backgrounds, they seem to be very keen on us obtaining the position of manager. This offered Jean and me not only more independence, but the flat above the wine bar, which was two storeys high, was something we could not afford to turn down.

The accountant: 'Can you both start next Monday morning?'

'That will be fine, thank you very much, but would it be okay if we moved in on Monday to get things straight and bring our bits and pieces?'

He replied, 'That would be fine, Bernard. We will give you the keys today as the wine lodge has been closed for several weeks.'

We were both very pleased, although I was a little disappointed about not taking the Savoy Hotel job; but with the flat going with the wine bar this was the best option. At about ten o'clock on Saturday morning, Jean and I let ourselves into the wine lodge. On opening the wine bar door, we just looked at each other and smiled. I remember Jean saying, 'It stinks a bit in here, doesn't it?' Which it did, of stale wine. The place was extremely dirty and looked as though it had been let go for many years.

We walked through the bar and at the far end

was a very big room with a pool table in the middle, the ladies and gents off to the left and right as well as a door to the cellar. When I opened the cellar door, I was amazed. There were probably about two dozen bottles of wine in there. The rest of the racks were empty. We went back to the bar, lifted the bar flap and, after going behind the counter, noticed the smell was really bad. Jean spotted a swab by the side of the sink which in actual fact was smoking. I picked it up and dropped it quickly as it was smouldering in the middle with internal combustion. Luckily enough we spotted it as it could have caused a fire. We both looked at each other in amazement.

The flat above was quite nice, actually, and not dirty; it looked as though they had had it decorated before they advertised the position for managers on the open market. All we had in the way of furniture was a double bed and two tea chests I got from a local shop, which Jean covered with gingham material; plus one table and two chairs which we borrowed. We went out and bought all our kitchen pots and pans that afternoon.

All day Sunday, we set about cleaning up the bar as best we could. It looked as though they only sold draft sherry which came in three-gallon plastic containers. I had worked out the cost price of buying in and set my percentages for the profit margin, for the management. The accountants gave me the address of different suppliers that they use.

It was about June when we took over as managers – quite nice weather actually. We wedged open the wine bar door at ten o'clock, waiting in anticipation for our first customer. Quite a few people stuck their heads round the door but did not come in, until about noon when two old people came in and bought two glasses of sherry. They introduced themselves as Flori and Albert. They seemed a couple of nice old people, questioning us quite a lot on our background, 'being nosy and curious at the same time'.

About half an hour later, in walked a man they called "Jimmy Windows", an extremely nice man – again ordering half a carafe of sweet sherry. A few minutes later a lady aged about sixty walked in and introduced herself, saying she was the cleaner and did I still want her? Yes, I said, but we will have to have a chat. She told me her name was Sally and she had a key to the main door. 'Okay Sally, I'll see you at eight tomorrow morning.' Needless to say, I had to inform her of the kind of cleanliness we both expected in the future. She bought a glass of sherry and sat down with Flo and Albert. They were talking very quietly to each other when in walked a man with extremely bushy curly hair looked as though he'd had a perm. This was Arnold whom they called Arnie. He was gay and extremely flamboyant in his mannerisms. And a very good friend, we gathered, of Sally's. All day we had exactly six customers.

Jean and I started from day one to try to improve the premises and get more customers in. There seemed to be a problem with the cash flow going from the accountants to the wine suppliers. So, Jean and I would use our own money to buy wine, then take off the *cost price and give the profit to the management at that particular time. We had no option really, we had to have something to sell. After a few months, trade began to increase and the accountants released more money for stock. They did apologise and said that they had quite a few managers who had ripped them off in the past, which had made them very cautious. But they were very pleased to see the way Jean and I had performed up to then.*

Needless to say, certain members of the public tried to take on Jean and me in the first few months of us taking over – testing us to see what we were made of. But we were both from the East End of London, and we were down the road and around the corner long before they got there. They soon realised we were no pushovers. We had our windows broken three or four times. Presumably by the unsavoury characters we had barred from the wine lodge. This thing of banning people, I might add, is quite usual. I mean, you get that quite a lot in the licensing game.

By this time, Colonel Hingston and his wife had made several visits to the wine lodge and were quite pleased with our performance. They were two lovely people whom we had the utmost respect for. Eventually, they sacked their accountants for inefficiency and took on new ones from the city. But they instructed them to let Jean and I run the business as we thought best, which was then paying dividends.

About two years later, they came in for lunch and a chat with both of us. Col. Hingston said he was selling off most of his London properties, and the wine lodge would be one of them. 'Would you be interested in renting or leasing this property, Bernard? Both my wife and I would love you and Jean to have it?' I was a little shocked at this news and said, 'With due respect, sir, I would not be interested in renting or leasing, but I would be interested in buying the freehold.' He looked at his wife with a big broad smile and then turned back to me. 'Bernard there is no better person I could wish to sell the freehold to but you and Jean. I'll give you a private mortgage. I'll see my solicitors and accountants tomorrow. I am delighted that you both would like to buy it.'

One week later, we met at Lincoln's Inn Fields to sign the legal agreements, making Jean and I the owners of the wine lodge. We borrowed money from the bank opposite. I then spent most of my time converting the premises back to Victoria times, putting in delicatessen counter and beautiful Victorian fixtures and fittings. We trebled the number of varieties of wine, from vintage Dom Pérignon to fine French and Italian wines, as well as others from around the world. And the gastronomic delights that we sold! Our trade went up and up. We were eventually doing approximately fifty lunches a day, just Jean and I and that doesn't include the food we sold in the evenings – from ham on the bone to ribs of beef, pastrami and a large selection of pâtés.

Chapter One

Bernard and Jean Hogan in the wine lodge, Upper Street, Islington, serving up Beaujolais Nouveau to Arthur Mullard and the Mayor of Islington.

My story begins. Michael, a customer, was sitting at the bar chatting to the landlady, Jean. He was with his girlfriend Rachel. Jean's partner, Bernard (that is me telling the story), was serving on the delicatessen counter. The bar was packed with people.

'Blimey Jean you're doing well tonight.'
'Well, it makes up for the slack times.'
'Don't give me that, you're making a bomb.'
'I wish!'

Above the noise of the customers was the clink of pool balls from a room at the back of the bar, where four or five out-of-work actors were playing pool with the manager of the London Palladium, Tony Pinhorn. Jean had just finished serving Jimmy Windows with half a carafe of sherry. Jimmy was a window cleaner as well as a steeplejack – one of his jobs was cleaning the face of Big Ben. God knows how he did it with all the sherry he drank. Jimmy walked over with his carafe to a table where "Flo" and "Elbert" was sitting. Two lovely old characters in their eighties.

'Care to join me?'

'We won't say no,' says Flo with a chuckle.

Flo and Elbert would sit there waiting for people to treat them. And Jimmy had a very kind heart. He sat chatting to Flo and Elbert for quite some time. Then the wine bar door quietly opened and an old man in his eighties stood there for a few seconds, stamped his walking stick on the floor and shouted out: 'Hoult the greys, steady the bays and let the artillery pass!' He was a lovely old gentleman we used to call the Italian man. He then sang a song: 'The Boers have got my daddy, my pride and joy,' (the song was about his father in the Boer war) when a voice shouts out, 'Sacré bleu! Can't we get any peace and quiet?' This comes from Lucienne, about 89 years old, wearing a hat dating back to the war years with about 6–8-inch-long hat pins sticking out of it. She was known to all of us as "The French cat with the hat". Lucienne was a lesbian and very proud of it. She would sit there for hours with a bottle of wine, reading Somerset Maughan and occasionally bursting out laughing when she came to an amusing piece.

I asked her one day what she did during the war. She said, 'I worked for the Mountbatten family as a housekeeper, and I did my bit for the war effort.'

'How's that, Lucienne?

'I slept with half the French Navy. Really.' (We were very fond of her, God bless her.)

Sitting in the other corner was Tony Fisk, a six-foot-tall gentle giant with huge hands. Tony did the first sawn-off shotgun bank raid in England. Tony had not long since come out of jail for passing $100 counterfeit notes for the Kray twins. He got thirteen years in a Spanish jail. But Franco the dictator had just died and King Carlos released all foreign prisoners, and Tony was one of them. He had done three years out of the thirteen they gave him. Tony knew all the villains in London, but three years in a Spanish jail had taken its toll.

He told me he only got water to wash with. 'It was undrinkable. They gave us very cheap watered-down wine to drink; hence we were all drunk or fuzzy in the head. Nobody escaped or even bothered.' Tony was now an angel. He was like our minder in the wine bar keeping all trouble away.

It was a Saturday night and I was chatting away to Michael and Rachel when Arthur Mullard walked in.

'Hi, Arthur, what you having?' said Michael.

'I'll 'ave a white wine mate. Blimey, that's cold out there tonight.'

'Got a vest on?' asked Michael

'Vest and the old Jonelles.'

Michael replied: 'Can't beat them I wear them behind the counter in the butcher's shop; we can't have heating in there.'

'Yeah, I bet that's bloody cold, mate. Enough to freeze the balls off a donkey.'

'We sell them as well.'

'Ha ha. Nice one,' said Arthur.

Later on in the evening, Arthur's friend Yootha Joyce came in. Both Jean and I liked her, she was a very nice lady with a good sense of humour. And quite a good friend of Arthur's. I left Jean chatting to Arthur and Yootha and went up to the pool room where Tony Pinhorn was playing pool with James Aubrey. James was a lovely lad whom I was very fond of. He played the leading role in the movie Lord of the Flies and was a member of the Royal Shakespeare Company. My stepdaughter Denise, who lived with us, accompanied me to the pool room.

'When you two guys have finished, me and Denise will take you both on.'

Tony said £5 a game. 'Feeling confident are we, Tony?'

'Yes, I think we're on a roll tonight. We'll take you to the cleaners.'

Fifteen minutes later, James racked up the

balls. We had a good evening. Denise and I took £20 off of them. Denise loved it as I used to give her all the winnings.

I walked down to the bar again and joined Jean who was still talking to Arthur and Mike and Rachel.

'Did they take you?' asked Mike.

'No, Mike, we took them to the cleaners… Denise is happy she's got twenty quid.

'Enough for three rounds of drinks.'

'You must be joking, Arthur. If anyone strangles the Queen, it is Denise.'

'Leave her alone bless her,' said Yootha.

With that, there was a chuckle from Lucienne, engrossed in her book.

'She seems to be enjoying that,' Mike said.

'You know she lives at Hampstead heath, and comes all this way to drink in the wine lodge. She's a lovely old lady. She leaves here usually as pissed as a newt. God knows how she gets home.'

'She's probably got a broomstick.'

'Come on, Mike, she is a lovely character.'

And with that, Mike bought her a glass of wine and took it over to her. She looked up from her book and said with a broad smile, 'Merci, Monsieur. Enchanté, Monsieur.'

'She said something in French,' said Mike.

'She was thanking you, Mike, for the drink and saying she was pleased to meet you.'

Mike smiled as he looked over towards her.

'Strange old girl.'

'No stranger than you, Mike.'

With that, the wine bar door opened and in walked Fingers Charlie with his two friends, Fred the Lloyd and Len 'the dipper'. Both Fingers Charlie and Len are what us Londoners call a dipper (pickpocket). Nick the Lloyd is a burglar using a plastic card.

Charlie looked over to the corner where Tony was sitting. They all knew Tony and treated him with the greatest of respect.

'Would you like a drink, Tone?'

'Yes, mate. I'll have a large sherry.

'Hello, Jean. When you gonna leave Bernard and run away with me?'

'Not just yet, Charlie, let's see the colour of your money for Tony's drink.'

'I'm brassic.'

'That'll be the day, Charlie. Stop messing about, and cough up.'

Half an hour later, Nancy walked into the bar. Nancy was once a Vogue magazine model. Quite an attractive lady, now in her fifties, who lived in a flat next door to the wine bar. She walked to the bar, and on seeing her, Len, who worked for the Evening Standard and was quite fond of Nancy, went over and picked her up with his arms around her waist.

'Put me down, Len.'

Also, Lucienne liked Nancy very much. On seeing this, she got up from her seat and walked towards Len, who had his back to her. It was incredible. I shall never forget it or the customers' reactions. She stood behind him as he held Nancy in his arms. And like a Spanish Matador withdrew a 6-inch hat pin and thrust it into Len's buttocks. I saw at least five inches disappear into this poor man's backside. He dropped Nancy, his face drained of colour and you could see he was in pain. Lucienne withdrew the lethal weapon, and calmly put it back into her hat and sat down to her drink.

Len, holding his buttock with one hand and turning round to face Lucienne, said, 'You shouldn't have done that.'

She replied, 'You do not treat a lady like that,' and calmly went on reading her book. The bar was in total silence while this took place, and then it was a buzz of chatter about what had happened. Jean and I did feel very sorry for Len.

'Blimey,' said Mike, 'I bet that was painful.'

'I should say so. But he can't do anything about it, she is an old lady.'

Len stood up for the rest of the evening chatting to Nancy and the rest of us. We all bought him drinks for the rest of the evening to ease the pain.

At 11 pm I locked the wine bar door to help the police keep law and order. The pubs closed in London at 11 to keep out the drunks from the pubs after they close. So, I locked the door. About midnight, there was a loud knock on the wine bar door. I lifted the bar counter flap and walked over and unlocked the door. Standing there was a police inspector, a sergeant, and a plainclothes officer. They walked into the bar, one policeman closing the bar door behind him and standing guard. The police inspector looked around the bar, which was packed with customers. Turning to me, he said, 'Are you the licensee of the premises?'

'Yes, inspector.'

'Are all these customers bonafide friends?'

'No, not all of them.'

'Well, Mr Hagon, under the licensing laws of this district you are committing an offence by selling alcohol past the allotted time which is 11 pm.'

'Without being impertinent, inspector, are you new in this area? Because I do not believe you are fully conversant with the law of this particular premises.'

He looked at me quizzically as though I was an idiot.

'With respect to you, inspector, if you go back to the police station and vet out the legality of these premises, you will find them unique. In other words, I have a royal charter dating 390 years back to Queen Anne. I do not need a licence to sell alcohol or to keep the allotted times laid down by the magistrates. The police, and Customs and Excise have no jurisdiction over me whatsoever. I have a royal charter. Only Her Majesty herself can tell me what to do. We are members of a London livery company.'

I continued. 'I know this might sound very strange to you but I can assure you I am telling you the truth; please make your investigation and you'll find I am telling you the truth. However, to help the police and also to keep law and order, I shut my bar door at eleven o'clock like all the pubs. But I do let my customers stay in the premises until one o'clock when I close. Please come in tomorrow and have lunch on my wife and me. We will be pleased to see you.'

The inspector then had a word with his sergeant. Then he said to me, 'I will come and see you Mr Hagon, tomorrow.'

'Thank you, Inspector, you will be welcome.'

He looked none too happy judging by the expression on his face as he left the wine bar. I expect he thought he had a 'collar' (a conviction). Time was ticking by now and it was nearly one o'clock. I shouted out, 'Time gentlemen, please,' and rang the bell. Walking up to the pool room, I said, 'Will you make that the last game, lads?'

Back at the counter, I said to Arthur, 'Would you and Yootha like to join Jean and me for an early bird breakfast at the Cavendish Hotel, at Jermyn Street, Mayfair, when we close? Jean and I often go there.'

'Love to, mate,' said Arthur.

'That sounds lovely, darling,' added Yootha.

'Not for me, Bernie,' said Mike. 'I've gotta get up early in the morning. Perhaps another time?'

Tony Pinhorn was standing at the counter, finishing his drink. 'Is there room for me Bernard?'

'Of course, Tony.' One more ring on the bell. 'Come on, ladies and gentlemen, haven't you got any homes to go to?' It took about another half an hour to clear the bar, allowing Jean and I to polish the glasses.

'Will you call a black cab, Jean? One will do; five of us can get in there.'

My stepdaughter Denise had already gone to bed as she had to be up for work early in the morning. There was a knock at the door; I answered it, and it was the black cab driver.

'You rung for a cab, mate.'

I locked up, we all piled into the cab. 'Cavendish Hotel please, mate.'

'Is that the one off Piccadilly Circus?'

'That's the one.'

On arriving at the hotel, I paid the cab driver and we walked to the entrance. The doorman, recognising Arthur and Yootha, made a little bow. We walked upstairs to the restaurant. There were quite a few people in there – actually more than usual.

'Table for five, Sir? If you'd like to follow me.'

Quite a few heads turned to look at us, recognising our company. I heard one woman say to her partner. 'That's Yootha Joyce with Arthur Mullard.'

We sat there and the waiter took our order. To Arthur: 'What would you like sir?'

'I'll 'ave a full English with two slices of fried bread.'

'Yes, and what would you like madam?'

'The devilled kidneys sound very nice. That will be fine.'

'Certainly, madam.'

Tony and Jean and I had a full English. 'Would you all like coffee or tea, sir?'

Arthur replied, 'I'd like a glass of red wine.'

'Brandy, please,' said Yootha.

'I'm sorry, we're not allowed to sell alcohol after hours unless you are a resident in the hotel. I'll consult the manager and see if he will make a concession.'

'Good' said Arthur.

Three minutes later the waiter came to the table and said, 'That will be okay, sir.'

'Right, I'll have a glass of red wine, and what are you having, Yootha?'

'Brandy please.' The rest of us had coffee. Yootha was telling us how unhappy she was. 'I have a basement flat in Paddington, Jean. I've had a brick through my window on quite a few occasions; it really is frightening. It's not all good being a celebrity. I just can't understand people doing things like this, and it puts me right on edge – consequently, I drink a lot.'

Arthur sympathised. 'I know exactly what you mean, I get quite a lot of abuse like you. I suppose it comes with the job.'

'That doesn't make it right though, does it?' said Jean

'There's not much we can do about it. You phone the police they take the details, but the little devils have gone by then.'

The waiter turned up at the table to take away the dirty plate, turning to Arthur.

'Was everything okay sir?'

'Andsome, mate.'

And you, Madam. Was everything okay?'

'Yes, thank you,' said Yootha.

We sat there with a cup of coffee and a pot of tea and had a good old chinwag. Tony, who was the manager of the London Palladium, was telling us about the problems he was having.

'At the moment, as you know, we have "The King And I", but that comes with its complications. Yul Brynner is not liked by the supporting cast in the show. As you know, he appears on stage, barefoot, in the role of the king. Somebody dropped a load of tintacks on the stage so he would tread on them. It caused an uproar. He was furious. We never found out who did it, but he is not liked at all. He is very bossy and wants everything his own way. Shame really that he has this attitude because he is such a good actor. People like Harry Secombe and Freddie Starr – everybody backstage and on stage just love them.'

Arthur agreed. 'I like Harry. I've been with

him on several occasions and he's not a bad bloke.'

'I believe you know my first wife's godmother, Arthur,' I said.

'You mean Mae West, Bernard? I was on stage with her at the Liverpool Empire in 1947 with your father-in-law David Davis. When she was born, David asked Mae to be godmother. I will never forget it. She said, "Of course, darling, I will be delighted." She was a fantastic character. Her wit was something out of this world and she couldn't care a crap if she pleased or offended. I just loved her. In those early days, I was a struggling actor...'

'Not now though, Arthur.'

'Ha ha. What upsets me now is my wife and I struggled to make ends meet for years bringing up two children, and she's not here to reap the benefits. She suffered very badly with depression and committed suicide.' We all went quiet for a few seconds. Then Yootha said, 'I still love you, Arthur.'

'Fanks, darling.'

'You're welcome.'

We all left the Cavendish, dropping off Yootha outside her flat in Sussex Gardens, Paddington. She was a little tipsy, but so were we all. We dropped Arthur off outside his flat off the Holloway Road. 'Drop us off at Marsden's Wine Lodge, Upper Street, please cabbie.'

Tony stayed in the cab and off he went.

'You left him to pay the cabby, Bernard.'
'Don't worry I'll give him a drink tomorrow.'

Chapter Two

By now, the wine bar was now doing extremely well and we were getting quite a name for ourselves. Upper Street, Islington, is an extremely busy location from the Holloway Road down to the Angel. Hence, we had a few people trying to open up wine bars around us. Witnessing the trade that we were having. I opposed each application in the Highbury Law Courts, Islington. It was getting ridiculous. We could not afford solicitors and barristers to fight on our behalf as we had a mortgage to pay. So, I conducted my own case each time. I opposed the applications myself in the court of law. I was advised and briefed by solicitors and barristers, who used our wine bar, as well as High Court judges, who showed me how to present my case. Following their instructions, I succeeded in winning five court appearances. And I must say I quite enjoyed it. My opening gambit, standing in the dock was: 'I beg the court's indulgence as I cannot manipulate the Queen's English like the Learned Gentleman on my right.' This kind of remark used to put a smile on the faces of my opponent and the court.

The judge's reply was: 'Do your best, Mr Hagon. You do have the court's indulgence.'

'Thank you, your honour.'

I was told the court leans favourably towards a layman conducting their own case. I lost one application for a liquor licence and that was to the Almeida Theatre down near the Angel, Islington, as that application had a great deal of public support. But that was not too bad because it was about one mile from the wine lodge.

The history and the magic of this lovely old wine lodge going back 390 years is really remarkable. Islington then was a small village in the middle of the countryside. Famous for its cattle supplying London for its milk, butter and cheese. I often wonder about the characters that used to use the wine lodge. Two hundred yards from the wine lodge in a recess between two buildings is a blue plaque on the wall saying this is where Mr Wilkins Micawber, out of Charles Dickens, used to live. To me, there is a hundred to one chance that Mr Micawber had been into my wine lodge sometime in his lifespan. Just like Dickens's characters, we had a similar clientele. From all walks of life. The Artful Dodger equals Fingers Charlie – there were even characters like Fagan. But I loved them all. To me, this was the London where I was born, just one mile away, in City Road.

We had been in the wine bar for about five years when one day a customer walked in; quite an impressive-looking character, about five foot three, extremely well dressed with a big handlebar moustache, looking somewhat like Terry Thomas. The lady with him was blonde, extremely attractive with a slim figure. He walked up to the counter with a big broad smile and said, 'I thought I would introduce myself and my wife. We have just taken over the management of The Compton Arms pub around the corner. My name is William and this is my wife Dorothy.'

He put his hand across the counter and we shook hands as I introduced Jean and myself. William spoke with a posh accent and so did his wife. Jean and I took a liking to both of them straight away. They seemed to be very nice people. And as time went on, we became very good friends, going out with each other for meals occasionally. A lot of my customers used their pub. They were referred to as "Wolly and Dotty" and they were very well-liked by all that met them.

One lunchtime, Fingers Charlie and his entourage came in, walked up to the counter and asked me if I'd heard about Wally and Dottie.

'No, what about them?' I replied.

'Both of them have done a runner with the week's takings.' They burst out laughing.

Jean and I looked at each other in astonishment.

'Wolly?'

'Yes, Bern, Wolly. I didn't think he had it in him, he was such a quiet bloke'

'We can't believe it either,' said Charlie. 'Charrington Brewery officials are around there now asking lots of questions about them. But I bet they're long gone now, Bern.'

About five months later, I got a telephone

call. I couldn't believe it. It was Wolly at the other end.

'Hi Bernard, I thought I'd give you and Jean a ring. I've just taken over management of the Pope's Grotto, Twickenham.'

'Blimey, Wolly, that's a fantastic pub. I know it well. Congratulations! Jean and I will pop out and see you.'

I turned to Jean and said, 'You won't believe it. That was Wolly on the phone. He's just taken over the Pope's Grotto in Twickenham. I know it well, Jean, it's one of the best pubs in London. They have waiters in tales and pinstripe trousers serving drinks at the table – that's how good it is. I didn't mention The Compton Arms, that would've been embarrassing. I can't believe he's just got in touch with us after all he's done. He's certainly got some front. I think we'll go out and see him just out of curiosity.'

Two weeks later, on a beautiful Sunday summer's day, we drove out to Twickenham. Pulling up outside the pub I could see it was packed out as usual. This pub was one of the best in London. I parked the car and Jean and I went in. There were four or five bar staff and it was very busy. I ordered a half-pint of Guinness and a sherry for Jean. I said to the barman, 'Could I see the manager, please? Tell him it's Bernard and Jean.'

'Okay, sir.'

We sat down at a table, and a little while

later, a man came up to the table and said, 'Excuse me, but you were asking after the manager.'

I said, 'Yes, William and Dorothy.'

He looked at me without a smile on his face and said, 'Do you know them?'

Straightaway, I knew something was wrong here.

'Yes, I know them. They had a pub around the corner from my wine bar in Islington. He rang me a couple of weeks ago to tell me he was the manager here.'

'That's right, he was. He and his wife ran off with the week's takings and we're trying to track them down.' I looked at Jean in astonishment. 'He's done it again.' The guy said, 'I'm the manager here now. What do you mean he's done it again?'

I then told him about The Compton Arms. He sat down and had a chat with us. I told our customers back at the wine bar about our little ride out. Some of them were astounded but Fingers Charlie just burst out laughing. 'The blokes got balls, Bernard.'

I remember one evening Jean had called time. I was playing pool with James Aubrey when I heard a few people shout out: 'Take it, Jean, take it!' I went down to investigate. There was a gentleman at the bar who I recognised; he had been in quite a few times.

He had asked Jean for a glass of wine, and she had refused, saying, 'I have already called time.' We were legally within our rights to serve him because of our unique position. A glass of wine then was 30p he had offered going up from a pound to eventually reaching £100 for a glass of wine. My Jean was very stubborn and said, 'I stopped serving five minutes ago and I'm sorry, you're too late.' With that the gentleman put down his glass and walked out of the bar with his friend, a furious look on his face, saying something in a foreign language that none of us understood. A few of the customers started to clap. One of our regulars, who was a newspaper reporter for the Observer London newspaper, said to Jean, 'Can I have that story?'

'What story?' said my Jean.

'You just turned down £100 for a 30p glass of wine. That's incredible!'

Jean walked away and carried on washing and polishing the glasses. The following midday, Michael Spence, son of Sir Basil Spence, who was a regular at lunchtimes, was sitting at the counter. He said, 'Congratulations, Jean.'

'What for?'

'You have won the Pendennis award in the Observer for your principles.'

'My principles?'

'Yes, you turned down £100 for a glass of wine, according to the paper.'

I said, 'Can I see that, Michael?' He handed

me the newspaper and there it was: 'Jean Hagon refuses £100 for a glass of wine after she had called time in Marsden's Wine Lodge, Upper Street, Islington. We congratulate her on her principles.' Needless to say, I was very proud of her.

'Well done,' said Michael.

A day later, a letter was delivered at midday addressed to Jean Hagon. It was a cream-coloured envelope with Her Majesty's Buckingham Palace coat of arms on it. Jean looked at me with a quizzical expression on her face.

'What is it, Jean?' She handed me the envelope without opening it. After seeing the coat of arms, I got quite excited. 'Please, you open it, Jean, it's addressed to you.' She opened the envelope and read the contents and with a smile on her face, she handed it to me. I held the letter with a shaky hand. I will say at this particular moment I have always been a royalist. I'm reading the content from Her Majesty the Queen congratulating Jean upon her principles. 'I can't believe it, Jean. A letter of congratulations from Her Majesty. That's bloody marvellous.'

I was so overwhelmed. With that, everybody in the bar burst out laughing. It was a wind-up because they knew how much I thought of the royal family. Jean couldn't stop laughing – she was in on it as well. Apparently, Peter Nielsen Bailey, Princess Margaret's equerry, who used the wine bar, furnished them with the envelope and the Buckingham Palace headed notepaper. This was the kind of camaraderie our customers had. It was lovely, and that joke was on me.

Two of our favourite customers were Benny and Don. Two lovely characters coming up to their seventies. Benny owned Dalston Motors, a former cinema which he gutted making an entrance for cars to drive inside where he would auction them off from the rostrum. Don was a retired wrestler who had wrestled internationally. He owned a chain of shops around London selling second-hand car parts. They were a couple of wealthy characters. With shady backgrounds. Benny was a Jewish gentleman with a big squadron leader's handlebar moustache. He was an incredible character, which Jean and I liked very much. He drove an Old American Pontiac car, and in the boot, he carried a sawn-off shotgun, which tells you something.

I remember one evening when they both came in, bought a drink and said, 'Would you like a long red carpet-runner for the wine bar, Bernard? We don't want anything for it, it's a present for you and Jean.

'Not really, Benny, we have too much traffic walking up and down plus spilt wine. Where has it come from?'

'Now that's a long story. Don and I went out for a drink last night up the West End. We ended up in the CAFE de Parry. When we came out, you walked down the long corridor. And there was a long red carpet running along it. Don said, "I like this, Benny, I think I'll have it." And with that, he rolled it all up, put it on his shoulder and we walk straight out. Chucked it in the back of the car and there we are.'

'You two are incredible; I don't know how you get away with it.'

'It's only a laugh, Bernard, no one hurt.'

One of our regular customers was Squadron Leader Victor Hogan. He used to run the motorbike exhibition at Earl's Court every year. He was a very highly decorated airman with ninety-one bombing missions over Germany where he lost one leg. In the early part of the war, he was a navigator for Bomber Harris when Bomber Harris was a pilot, before he came head of Bomber Command. He was a very nice gentleman, very well-spoken and very kind. He had a soft spot for my Jean, I overheard him telling her one day how upset he was.

'Jean, I've been running the Earl's Court motorcycle exhibition for quite a number of years; each year I give away six motorcycles in raffles, and so on. And I am lucky if I get one person to say thank you. I just can't understand some of these people today.'

One particular morning, Victor came in, put his walking stick on the counter and looked as though he was in pain. I said, 'Are you okay

Victor?'

'Not really, Bernard. I've just got a new artificial leg and it's chafing very badly, it's not a proper fit. It's rubbing just here by the side of my knee.'

'Can you take it off, Victor? I may be able to take a little piece off where it's rubbing.' With that, he sat down, rolled up his trouser leg, unstrapped the prosthetic leg and handed it to me. I looked at the side of his knee and could see that it was quite sore. I got a half-round bastard file and filed a small piece off the inside of the fibreglass where it was rubbing, then sanded it down with some fine sandpaper. This I did, believe it or not, behind the counter with his leg tucked underneath my arm with the sock and his shoe attached to it. It caused quite a bit of amusement in the bar among some of his friends. I rubbed a little Vaseline on the part I had removed then wiped it clean with a piece of cloth and handed it back to him. He strapped it back on, got up from the table and walked up and down.

'Bernard, thank you, it feels much better.'
'Victor, it was a pleasure.'

Chapter Three

One day, the Dean of RADA came in and said, 'I wonder if you would do me a favour, Bernard.'

'What is it?'

'We are making a film, and we're on a very strict budget of £700. And I was wondering if we could use the wine bar in one of the screenshots. For nothing.'

'Of course you can, but it will have to be on a Sunday when we are closed. Is that alright with you?'

'That would be brilliant Bernard.'

'What is the name of the film?'

'It's called Unknown Woman. Will this coming Sunday be okay, say around nine o'clock, if that's okay with you Bernard?'

At nine o'clock on Sunday morning, there was a knock on the door which I opened to see large unmarked pantechnicon removal vans pulled up outside. They were followed by about six cars which drew up behind them. Two men stapled white sheeting over the outside window to the wine bar. Then two giant floodlights were placed on the pavement, shining onto the white sheets. I said to the guys, 'What's that for?' and they said that when you're inside the building it looks like sunshine through the windows. While that was going on, three men were laying down small railway lines running through the bar. Large camera equipment was placed on a trolley. That went up and down the lines running very smoothly.

The director said, 'This is going to be a bar scene, of course, Bernard. Would you like to be the barman in the movie? Just be yourself and serve as you would every day.'

'I'd be delighted, thank you very much.'

The filming went quite well and lasted till about five o'clock in the afternoon. Jean and I were invited to a theatre in Piccadilly to the premier. It was quite exciting for me to see myself in a movie. I was billed in the credits as the sinister barman, which made Jean laugh. The movie was quite good and we really enjoyed it, considering it was done by students.

This was the third time the wine lodge had been hired for filming. The year before, LWT came to see me and asked permission to film a scene in the wine lodge for the series called *The Professionals* featuring Lewis Collins and Martin Shaw as Bodie and Doyle, with Gordon Jackson. They said they would come on the day we were closed and would pay me £700 for the day's hiring. Seven hundred quid sounded good to me, plus it was very good publicity for the wine lodge. As before, the film team arrived early Sunday morning bringing in all the equipment, but they needed loads of lighting with tons of cables running to a van with a giant generator in it.

It was quite nice meeting the cast. Gordon

Jackson was a really lovely guy and that particular day was his birthday, so there were drinks all round after the production. They spent nearly the whole day there, so Jean and I had quite long talks with Gordon. Quite a few people gathered outside in the street watching what was going on and waiting to see Gordon Jackson and the cast.

Jimmy Windows with his ever-present carafe of sherry, one of the real London characters who were regulars at Marsden's Wine Lodge in Islington.

The same year, 1986, a film company had the wine bar to film the Philip Marlowe, Private Eye series starring Powers Boothe. He was quite a nice guy, again we spent the whole day with him. I suppose Jean and I were getting quite blasé because of meeting so many famous people over the years we were there.

But at the end of the day, they are all the same as you and I; they have their problems, their ups and the downs. But out of all our customers, the ones I like best are the Jimmy Windows, Fingers Charlie, The French Cat with the Hat personalities; these are the real London characters. We had the wine bar for fifteen years – an uphill climb in the beginning. Like rolling a boulder up a hill, it is a struggle till you reach the pinnacle and then it is downhill all the way. That applies to every business. "Quality first then profits will follow." We both concentrated on the little things. To quote Michelangelo: 'Trifles make perfection, and perfection is no trifle.'

Some Sundays I would go down to Chapel Market to help my friend Colour Sergeant Major Sam Roberts and his wife Renée on their shoe stall. This was a great pleasure. I thoroughly enjoyed all the banter from the stallholders to the general public; it was London to me. To see these ladies walk by and shout out to them: 'Come on, darling, come over here, I've just got a pair of shoes that really will suit you. They used to come over out of curiosity with a smile on their face.

'Ere, darling, try these on lovely pair of "hi hills". They are bloody cheap as well. Cor blimey, they don't half suit you. Give us six quid. Quick before I change my mind.'

I used to love it. Especially the old pie and mash shop, Manze's. The Reverend Ronnie from Union Chapel used to come in every day for quite a few glasses of sherry. He was a lovely vicar with a very kind heart and much respected in Islington. I'm afraid his demise was to fall down the steps of the Union Chapel after having one too many and breaking his neck.

Two of our regular customers, Ted and Thelma, owned a large house in Canonbury Georgian Gardens, and turned it into a small hotel, come boarding house. A very nice establishment. We had a new customer that had been in the wine lodge three or four times, extremely well dressed and spoke with a polished English accent. We got to know him and thought he was a lovely character, a thorough gentleman. He said he was educated at Cambridge University and was a film director come actor at the moment doing some work for The Royal Academy of Arts. Over the few weeks we got to like him very much. It was on about the fourth week he invited Ted, Thelma, Jean and I out for dinner one evening when it was convenient for us, as he was celebrating a film contract with MGM, and would like us to accompany him as his guests. By this time he had checked in to Ted and Thelma's hotel It was on a Friday evening we had decided to go, my mother-in-law Daisy and my mother were running the wine lodge in our absence. Peter Sinclair Ford, Peter as we called him, turned up at the wine lodge at 6:30. Ted and Thelma were already there. A black cab arrived not long after and off we went to this mystery restaurant. I could see that we were heading for the West End and to our surprise we pulled up outside the Savoy Hotel. " Blimey Peter you are pushing the boat out." " Nothing but the best for you lovely people with my compliments."

Peter walked in front and we followed behind. He stood for a few moments talking to the Maitre D who then escorted us to our table. Peter said" order what you like this is a special occasion." The sommelier came to the table and asked what wine we would like. We decided we all liked red so we had two bottles of Bordeaux. Peter ordered Scottish fillet steak, Ted and I had the same, I forget what the girls had, but it was a lovely evening.Peter talked quite a lot about the acting business and a good time was had by all. We were having coffee at the table, Peter left to go to the toilet, we chatted for quite a while and then realised Peter had been gone for some time, a good twenty minutes to half an hour. I got up from the table and asked the sommelier if he had seen the gentleman sitting at a table. He said yes he saw the gentleman leaving about half an hour ago. I said" Have you seen this gentleman before?". He replied" "No is there a problem sir. " Yes he invited us here this evening for a meal" "Oh sir the gentleman has made a hasty retreat I take it." " He certainly has, leaving us to pay the bill." "I am sorry sir." " Thank you." With that I returned to the table. Looking at Ted I said "We've been done Ted". "You mean he's done a runner," "Definitely." We all looked at each other and burst out laughing as we were left to pay the bill between us. I said to Ted" I wonder if he's gone back to your hotel?"" That's a point Bernard. He's been with me for over a week, I'll put money on it we won't see him again."

Later that evening when we got home Ted rang me and said he'd let himself into Peter's room there was a suitcase but it was empty.

Well, the years rolled by. One weekday, a gentleman who had been in the wine bar on several occasions, lunchtime and evening, walked in and ordered a glass of wine sitting down at the counter. He was a foreign gentleman – I imagined Egyptian, but I found out later he was Algerian.

'Do you own this wine bar, Bernard?'

'Yes, Jean and I own the freehold. Why do you ask?'

'Would you be interested in selling?'

'I suppose so if the price was right.'

He opened his wallet and got out one of his cards, wrote on the back of it and then passed it over the counter to me. I looked at it and tried not to gulp or give an expression of any kind.

'Come and see me tomorrow, I'll have a word with Jean.'

That evening Jean and I discussed the offer he had made. 'Let's take it, Bernard. It is too big to refuse.' The following day he came in again for lunch. I said, 'Based on the figure you gave me, it's a deal. I will get in touch with my solicitor, David Marcus; his offices are three doors up from here. This is his address and telephone number.'

We both shook hands over the counter and I opened a bottle of champagne to toast the transaction. Needless to say, our customers, who had become our friends, were so disappointed at hearing the news.

Chapter Four

After selling up, we moved in with my mum in Bermondsey and started to look around for somewhere to live. We decided to go and visit an old friend of ours, Freddie Gun, who had moved to Wroxham in Norfolk. It was a beautiful summer's day as we motored down there in the Triumph Stag with the roof off.

Freddie's house was on the side of the river – a beautiful bungalow. Fred was a retired managing director of A1 Packaging, a plastics company in London, and he was so pleased to see us. At the bottom of his garden was the river; he had a lovely Freeman six-berth motor cruiser. Freddie put a case of tonic waters in the back, two bottles of gin and plenty of ice. And off we went down the river towards Horning.

As we approached it, on the corner was an old English pub, The Swan; alongside was the village green, and at that particular moment there was the village carnival on the green with a maypole, music and stalls. It was most picturesque and straightaway my Jean said this is where I want to live. And this is where we have been for thirty-eight years. One of the happiest times of my life with my dear wife, who has now passed away, leaving a big hole in my life.

We bought a lovely chalet bungalow in a cul-de-sac with nothing else but rolling fields all around us. It felt like we had both died and gone to heaven. After one month of settling in, we bought a 23-foot Freeman cabin cruiser that would sleep six people. I paid for a mooring not far from the bottom of my road. Our house was always packed out with people every weekend with customers from our wine bar staying over and also my brother-in-law Hans and Ivy, my wife's sister, plus, her two daughters Andrea and Elke, all arriving from Germany.

After two years of not working, I got restless and decided to look for a job at one of the local boatbuilders. They took me on immediately after hearing that in my younger days I worked in a boatbuilders' yard on Canvey Island, Essex, making clinker-built wooden sailing cruisers. I worked there for three years until I was made redundant due to the lack of work. Then, one day, driving into Norwich, I saw a beautiful old mansion being restored into a beautiful old hotel. It was called Sprowston Manor. I decided to drive down this beautiful long driveway to the hotel. The place at the time was full of workmen, but the old part of the hotel was still open. I enquired at the desk. 'Are there any jobs going here in the hotel?' The reply came: 'If you'd like to take a seat, I'll ring the manager."

So, I sat down for about a quarter of an hour when an attractive young lady, about 30 years old, approached me.

'Good morning, my name is Paula. I am the

assistant manager and I hear you are looking for a job here in the hotel.'

'That is correct, ma'am.'

'Have you any experience in the hotel industry?'

'Quite a lot. I went to catering sea training school and sailed on luxury liners for thirteen years going through many catering departments.'

She ordered coffee for two and we had a very good conversation she was a charming young lady and I felt she was very professional, which I admire.

'Our official opening is not for another three weeks, Bernard. Can I call you Bernard?'

'Of course, ma'am.'

She smiled and said, 'In private, you can call me Paula.'

'Thank you. Does that mean I have a job?'

'You can start on Monday in conference and banqueting, who will fit you out with a uniform. Monday morning at eight o'clock.'

'Thank you very much, Paula.'

With that, we shook hands and I departed feeling quite pleased as this was going to be another adventure in my life.

I arrived at seven o'clock on Monday morning, reporting to the front desk. They found the conference and banqueting manager who introduced himself and took me upstairs to be measured for a tailor-made uniform. He said, 'In the meantime, Bernard, would you muck in with us or help to get rid of all the old hotel clutter, those fixtures and furniture we wish to get rid of. There is so much of it down in Davy Jones's locker.' This was the cellar under the building.

'Of course, no problem; just guide me in the right direction.'

It was incredible the beautiful stuff they were getting rid of, like early Victorian chandeliers that were just thrown into old tea chests. Lovely old paintings were being put into the cellar underneath the building. I asked if I could purchase any of these. The manager was consulted and said 'make us an offer', which I did and purchased six paintings. Four I still have today, the other two I put up at auction. The chandeliers were to go into a large skip container to be thrown away.

I asked the general manager if I could have them and his answer was: 'As long as they're off the premises, I don't care where they go.'

'Thank you, John, I'll take them home. And rebuild them.'

'I don't care what you do with them, Bernard. Just get them off the premises.' I spent three weeks in my spare time cleaning, rewiring and sorting out all the bits and pieces to make one chandelier. I put it in the local auction rooms and it fetched £490. Not bad for something that was going to be thrown away!

Conference and banqueting was a quite interesting field to work in. Most of our customers were from Norwich Union (now Aviva), and I got to know the lecturers extremely well as they were here nearly every week. It was the end of December 1990 when we officially opened the new building, and I must say I was very impressed at the quality and the taste that was chosen for this beautiful old mansion. It was finished in the late Victorian style. In previous years, I spent my service at sea in some of the biggest and most luxurious liners afloat in those days. This hotel now came up to their standards under the guidance of Mr and Mrs Spurrier, who had exquisite taste. It was a pleasure to work for them.

After a short period of time, our general manager Mr John Cotter called me into the office and asked me to become the concierge on reception, meeting and greeting the customers. Also, I was asked to be the master of ceremonies at weddings and functions, and a few after-dinner speeches. All this I thoroughly enjoyed. I emceed more than a thousand weddings, but my biggest was the granddaughter of Isoroku Yamamoto, the Japanese Admiral who led the attack on Pearl Harbour. His granddaughter married an English squadron leader. What a fantastic wedding it was! Her father paid for a jumbo jet to fly from Japan to Norwich Airport with all the Japanese guests. Two days after the wedding he flew all the guests to Paris for a week at his expense.

At the wedding table, he handed me an

envelope to present to the bride and groom. As she opened it, she looked astonished, looked at her husband and handed him the contents. The bride was a nurse in a Tokyo hospital and her father had brought her two hospitals as a wedding present – one on the outskirts of Tokyo. They were a lovely couple.

Six years later, I was standing at reception when a young Japanese lady walked through the door with two beautiful girls around six years old. She walked up to me and said, 'Do you remember me?'

'Ma'am, how could I forget such a beautiful bride?'

'I'm glad to see you, Bernard,' she said.

'Thank you, ma'am.'

After that, the following year, I acted as butler for Charlton Heston, Sir Harry Secombe and got to wait on many famous people, including Sir Robert and Lady Sainsbury, who I became very friendly with. My wife Jean and I were given a written invitation by Lady Sainsbury to their inauguration, having been given the Freedom of the City of Norwich. They also made my wife and me lifelong members of the Arts Society of Great Britain, which was a beautiful present. They came to the hotel every year in the summer for three weeks to visit the University of East Anglia, which was very close to their heart, and of course, as you all know, they virtually built a whole university. Their generosity goes without saying. Two of the most likeable people I have ever met and their generosity to this country was stupendous. The last time I saw Lady Sainsbury, she was being wheeled through the main reception by her nurse. She looked at me with a big broad smile and held out a red ribbon with a beautiful medal at the end of it.

'What a pleasure it is to see you, Lady Sainsbury,' I said

Holding the medal in her hand and with a smile on her face, she replied, 'This is the Order of the Rising Sun presented to me by the Emperor of Japan.'

'What can I say, ma'am? An extreme honour, you must be very proud.' So, Robert had passed away a few years before, and this was the last time I was to see her. God bless their memory.

A couple of years later I was called up into the general manager's office. 'Do take a seat, Bernard.'

'Is there a problem sir?'

'No, Bernard, but what I am about to tell you now must stay in these four walls. Have I your word?'

'Of course, sir.'

'In three weeks' time, we have an extremely important guest coming to the hotel to stay for three days. I cannot tell you who it is at this present time, for security reasons, but I would like you to be the butler for these guests, knowing that you know protocol better than any of us.'

'Thank you, sir, it would be a privilege.'

'I'll tell you, Bernard, nearer the time what day they will be arriving. You will have to be vetted by the Home Office.'

'With respect sir, I am already on their books. I have at one time in my life signed the Official Secrets Act.'

'You never seem to amaze me, Bernard.'

'Just one of those things, sir.'

Needless to say, the rumours started to fly around the hotel. One was that it was the Emperor of Japan who was staying. I told my wife Jean all about it and that I would not be coming home for three days as I would be staying at the hotel. And I had to be at the beck and call of these people all the time, day and night. On the morning of their arrival I was told by the manager it was the King and Queen of Malaysia and their entourage. We had rolled out a long red carpet from the main entrance to where the limousine would park. I was asked to stand by the door.

'You will be the only one to greet Their Majesties, Bernard. Just three of us, the heads of department, will stand in a line and you will introduce Their Majesties to us and then escort them to the Gainsborough Suite. Once they have settled in, liaise with us, Bernard, and keep us in the picture regarding their requirements.'

From the main entrance, I could see straight up the driveway. There was a four-police motorcycle escort leading, behind them a Daimler and behind that, a Rolls-Royce followed by more vehicles. The police motorcyclists pulled up at a distance from the main entrance; the Daimler stopped short of the main entrance and the security men got out very quickly and moved to the side of the red carpet. The Rolls-Royce pulled up in front of the main entrance. One of the security guards moved forward swiftly and opened the rear door for His Majesty the King, who got out followed by Her Majesty the Queen. I instinctively bowed, not looking directly at his face but at his chest. Looking directly eye to eye is considered discourteous, so I followed all the right formalities.

I said, 'Welcome Your Majesties to Sprowston Manor.' They both smiled and I continued, 'Allow me to introduce you to our general manager and his staff.' I introduced them one by one and waited for them to have a brief conversation, after which I said, 'Allow me to escort Your Majesties to your suite.' We arrived at the Gainsborough Suite, I slipped off my shoes and opened the door standing inside with my head bowed. They both inspected the suite and His Majesty returned to where I was standing.

'Are there any light refreshments Your Majesties would like?'

'What is your name?'

'Bernard, Your Majesty.'

'Then that is what I'll call you.'

'Thank you, Your Majesty. I shall be outside your room day and night, Your Majesty for anything you require.'

'Thank you, Bernard.'

With that, I walked backwards to the door closing it behind me. They were over here to look over Lotus Cars as they were the main shareholders of the company. They ordered dinner to be served in the room. I waited at table for them, serving coffee when they had finished. I cleared away the table and walked backwards to the door, giving a slight bow. After about an hour sitting outside their room, one of their security officers came up to me and said: 'That will be okay now, Bernard. Go and take a break, and I will stand guard.'

When he bent forward, I could see this gentleman had a gun in a holster under his jacket. There were two of these guys – they were quite pleasant actually and very polite – also His Majesty's aide-de-camp.

They had a banquet in our main ballroom the following evening. We had to get people in to erect a platform for their table to be put on as by tradition their heads must be higher than the guests. We had the Lord Mayor of Norwich and loads of lords and ladies came down from London to attend the banquet. Again, I was the only one allowed to be near them and serve them. It was quite an experience one that I shall never forget.

On the third day, when they were about to

depart, I was called to the suite. Their Majesties stood there, side-by-side.

'You called, Your Majesty?'

'Yes, Bernard. Her Majesty and I are very pleased with you and we would like you to accept this gift to say thank you.'

With that, he handed me an oblong box. With my head bowed, I said, 'It has been an honour and a privilege to serve Your Majesties.' And then I walked backwards out of the room. All the staff including the manager, said, 'Open the box, Bernard. Let us see what you have.'

'I said, 'I'm sorry, but I'm only going to open it in front of my wife. I'll tell you all tomorrow and bring it in whatever it is.'

When I got home I showed the box to Jean. 'Well open it then!' she said. We did so, and there was a Pierre Renoir gold watch with four diamonds in it and His Majesty's name written across the face. But it didn't end there.

I was invited by the Crown Prince to go to Kuala Lumpur and visit the royal family on my way to Australia to see my son, who lives there. We did this the following year. We were met at the airport by a chauffeur-driven Rolls-Royce to take us back to the hotel. The chauffeur told us he would be our chauffeur the whole time we were there. 'I will be parked in front of the hotel day and night if there is anywhere you wish to go.'

That same evening, we were invited to the royal golf course where His Majesty and the

family were having dinner in the banqueting suite.
It was incredible; it was just like dining with any
ordinary big family. They talked about the children
at school and university and the normal things
that we would talk about around our own tables.
Their Majesties made us very, very welcome. After
the meal, the Crown Prince said, 'You and Jean
follow me, Bernard.' We went through the side
door downstairs into the basement which was
really a nightclub. We sat down at a table and a
waiter come running over bowing to the Crown
Prince and speaking to him in Indonesian.

'What would you and Jean like to drink,
Bernard?' We ordered and sat there for about
fifteen minutes when a slim medium-sized
gentleman, around 5 ft 4 ins I estimate, came up
to the table with a big smile and spoke to His
Highness. Immediately, His Highness said, 'Allow
me to introduce you and Jean, this is our Prime
Minister.' Looking back, it seems like a dream that
this kind of thing could happen in our life.

Back at the hotel, Jean said to me: 'Please
Bernard, in future can't you meet ordinary people?
All I want to do is shop.' But it didn't just stop
there. The King and Queen who were both in their
70s and 80s died, and when the next Malaysian
monarchs came to Norfolk to inspect Lotus Cars,
they personally requested that I was to be their
butler.

I could carry on and tell you more, but if you
like what I have written up to now, you can get a

copy of my autobiography and read all about my amazing life. It is called *Written While I Can Still Remember* and is available on Amazon books.

Chapter Five

I will now revert back to just three years ago. Michael my friend from the wine bar had contracted cancer and was dying. He phoned me and said he had not got long to go and wanted me to come up to Luton to see him. His flat was off the main drag. A downstairs one-bedroom flat consisting of lounge, kitchen and bathroom with a little garden. I knocked at the door but it was partly open. A faint voice from inside said, 'Come in.' Michael had his bed in the front room made up, but he was sitting in his armchair.

'Lovely to see you, Bernard, thank you for coming.'

'Don't be silly, Michael, it's a pleasure, my old friend.' He had lost a lot of weight and looked very pale and drawn.

'Make yourself a cup of tea, Bernard. Sorry I can't give you any of the hard stuff as I stopped drinking quite a while ago.'

'That's okay, Mike, no problem. Tea will do me nicely.'

After asking me a lot of questions about the passing of Jean and how I was coping without her, he said he was the biggest fool on this Earth to have lost Rachel.

'I treated her badly, Bernard. No wonder she left me in the early days of the wine bar. But there it is I can't turn the clock back. After she left me I turned to a life of crime. As you know, I was running a blue film cinema in Clerkenwell for a friend, but I was skimming off the top, Bernard, I was earning really well. And he hadn't a clue. You and Jean had sold the wine bar then and were living in Norfolk. I really envy you both. You had each other, a nice bungalow and a few bob in the bank. Something I suppose I was always looking for. Do you remember you hadn't heard from me for over a year, and I found you from Argentina?'

'I remember Mike.'

'Well, it was like this. I went to work for the biggest car dealership in London as a car salesman. The wages were poor but I got a commission on each car I sold, which wasn't bad. There were six of us salesman and a manager. We were selling ten to fifteen cars a week. We were making more money on hire purchase then by selling them for cash. The firm was earning most of its money from the commission from the hire purchase companies. But people still had to put down a deposit round about £1500 to £2000. This worked out roughly that there was about £100,000 going into the safe once a week, which the manager paid in on Monday mornings. The opportunity made me dribble, Bernard.'

He continued. 'So, I worked out a plan of action. We had security lights and also security cameras concentrating on the cars. I worked out the blackspots accordingly. I'm sitting in the office this day when one of the salesmen came in with this guy who was buying this car. They sat down and did the paperwork and the customer handed over the deposit to the salesman. He then gave it to the sales manager who signed the receipt book with the salesman. The manager then walked over to where all the security keys were hanging, taking one and then opening this huge safe, depositing the cash inside then locking it and replacing the keys on the hook with the rest. Bernard, I was amazed at the slapdash security. Man, it was a golden opportunity I couldn't give up.

'I spoke to the geezer I know in Clerkenwell who could cut keys. I bided my time till there was a golden opportunity of me being left in the office alone. I took a tobacco tin which I filled with plasticine; took an impression of the safe key and the door key to the office. I gave the impressions to my mate in Clerkenwell. He made me two keys. I waited one day to be alone in the office and tried them both. It was brilliant, they both fitted perfectly. And it only cost me 200 quid.

'It was one Saturday night pissing down with rain. This was just the job as not many people would be milling around and those that were would be hurrying to get out of the rain and not looking around at other people. It was eleven o'clock at night. I chose this time because if it was later in the evening there wouldn't be many people on the streets and to avoid the Old Bill patrolling in their cars. I made sure to keep out of the line of fire from the cameras just in case I would be recognised. I've got over the fence and crouching down low made my way to the office.

Unlocked it and walked in. Believe it or not, no security cameras were ever put inside the office. Bloody fools. I open the safe with the key. And there it was, just under 100 grand. I didn't stop to count it, I stuffed it into a backpack and slung it over my shoulders. Locked the safe. Looked out the window to see if all was clear, locking the front door as I left. Bernard, I could not believe how easy it was.

'On the Monday morning, I went to work as normal. All was quiet until the manager opened the safe to collect the week's takings and pay it into the bank. He called us all into the office. His face was as red as a beetroot. I think his blood pressure was ready to blow, and he was shaking. He did not like the head salesman called Tony at all, and he was the last one to pay in any money. He accused Tony in front of all of us. And suspended him straight away. After interrogating him, the manager then phoned the owner and broke the bad news. Three people came and questioned us all. There must've been something fishy going on, Bernard, with the company as they didn't call the police in on this.

'I carried on working there for another two months to cover any suspicion that I was involved. You could cut the atmosphere with a knife over that period. And the manager got the sack a few weeks later. About four weeks after I left, I booked a flight to Argentina, stayed there for four weeks and rang you from there. Remember, I told you at the time I was on holiday, but that was not the truth. I was going round the world living like a king. It was bloody marvellous.'

As I said previously, he poured his heart out to me regarding his past. Telling me of all his crimes in life. I have a feeling it was like a confession getting it off his chest before he passed on, which was three days after my visit.

Mike carried on with his story. 'But can you believe this? About a year passed by and I still had the keys. I thought of all that money just lying there waiting for me to take it again. So, shit or bust, I done it again. Not quite so much in the safe this time, but still a tidy old screw. So, I semi-retired for a little while, taking a few holidays to the Costa del Sol. And staying at the Ritz Carlton Tenerife. Living like a lord. And I bought myself a very nice 1982 Mercedes SL. Coupe. Metallic blue. Although it was old it was in pretty good condition so I had it renovated. Bern, it was the bee's knees. One year went by. As you know, like you I love jazz. So, I use this Irish pub not far from Islington. I think I took you and Jean there once to listen to some jazz when you had the wine bar years ago.'

'I can remember, Mike, some very good jazz musicians, and if I can remember, it was really packed.'

'It's always like that, Bern. They have ten or twelve barmen behind the counter to cope with the trade. It was about eleven o'clock on a

Monday morning and I was having a quick pint in there. It was very quiet, not many people about when this guy walked up to the counter carrying a small suitcase chained to his left hand. He was about six foot one and built like a brick shithouse, very well dressed in his late forties and had a very expensive pale grey whistle and flute. Not the kind of guy you wanna mess with.

'He plonked the case on the counter. One of the barmen called the manager who came down with a large safe deposit box under his arm and carrying a ledger in the other hand. He smiled and greeted the big guy. I was too far away to hear what they were saying. The manager put the book on the counter, opened it at a certain page and turned the book round for the geezer to look at. They both signed the book and the manager opened the deposit box on the counter. He looked as though he was counting the contents but not removing them. So, I couldn't see what he was counting. He then signed the book and so did the manager. He unlocked his case on the counter and put the contents of the safe deposit box into his case. I still couldn't see what he was putting in the case as the lid remained upright blocking my view. Looking back now, I think that was on purpose. A few more words took place and then the bloke left without having a drink.

'I said to myself, "That's interesting, he has just come in to collect the week's takings." I kept on thinking about that all morning and all day. So,

I decided I would go in every Monday morning about the same time to check on this guy to see if his habits and his timekeeping were always the same. Two weeks later, instead of going in the pub, I parked my car a little distance from the entrance of the pub. The bloke was a man of habit, Bernard, dead on time, locking his car before he went into the pub. I waited till he came out. He went up to the passenger side lifted the front seat and locked something underneath with a key on his keyring. This I saw through a pair of binoculars, as I didn't want to be too close to the car as I might be seen. He then put down the seat, locked the door, went round to the driver's side and drove off. I followed him at a safe distance. About twenty minutes later, he pulled up outside another Irish pub and went in. I waited half an hour at a safe distance, clocking his time and writing it down in my book. Out he came and did exactly the same as he did at the last pub. In all, he visited four pubs doing exactly the same thing.

'I thought to myself, "Michael, there must be a bloody fortune there underneath that car seat." I carried on going to the same pub at eleven o'clock every Monday morning for a pint, staying a safe distance away from where the bloke did his collection. I did this for three months, following him on some occasions to check his timings and his habits. I didn't go into any of the other pubs during the day, but I did some evenings, mostly on a Saturday night when they were packed, to see how the trade was. One thing, Bernard, I'm not telling you the names of these pubs.'

'Okay, Mike, I understand.'

'All this time I'm working out in my head a plan of action that must be done in fine detail if I'm going to pull this off successfully. No room for mistakes. I decided that it would take three of us to safely pull this job off. The beauty of this is we are unknown, not a member of one of the London mobs. And they will probably take the blame. This is the reason I've kept "schtum" all these years as to what happened. The two guys that helped me have both passed on. One had a fatal car accident. And the other one had cancer like me. So, I suppose we'll get to meet each other upstairs, or should I say "downstairs". Either way, they did well out of it. I told them in the beginning when they signed up, "This is my job, I've planned it, you're just helping me. I'll be fair to you, I'll pay you 40 per cent; this will be split between the two of you. Your decision." They asked me roughly how much their 40 per cent would be. "I don't know for sure, but I reckon roughly about £160,000. Are you in or out? Take it or leave it."

'Without hesitation, Bern, they said they were in. I knew they were both brassic and needed the dough. Plus, I trusted them and I've known them for quite a few years – both sensible blokes not idiots. I drove out to a B&Q in Chingford to park the car, about ten minutes' walk away, I disguised myself, walked up to the tools department, picked up a pair of bolt cutters and took them to the checkout. And paid for them with cash. Chingford is well off my manor. Can't be too careful can you, Bernard? I needed three pairs of rubber gloves, which I bought locally. I now needed an oxyacetylene torch and welding kit, which I bought off the internet second-hand from a grubby backstreet garage that had gone tits up. I hired a plain white van, stuck on some false number plates and picked up the gear. Paying the guy cash.

'A friend of mine, who lived in a block of council flats in Camden, had a garage underneath the flats he lived in. He didn't have a car so I asked him if I could rent the lock-up garage to put my Mercedes in and gave him £10 a week. He was well pleased. But he didn't know what I really wanted it for. I drove the van down to Camden and put the welding gear with the bottles in the garage and locked it up. I told my two helpers now exactly what the job was, but I didn't tell them where it was. I chose another pub in London and took the boys with me to simulate exactly what I wanted them to do. Call it a rehearsal. We done this three times to get it exactly right.

'One Saturday, I was drinking in the pub which was packed out with Irish guys and it dawned on me: in two months' time, on a Saturday, it was Saint Patrick's Day. This pub and the other three are going to be packed out with drunken Irishman. Spending money like water. I said to myself, "Michael that's the time to do the job. On the Monday, the takings will be way over the top of a normal week." I took the boys out for a drink and told them of my plan of action. "Once we've done the job, we won't split the money till three months after" They didn't look pleased. But I said, "This is for your own good and mine as well. The temptation will be there for you to splash the cash around and this will draw attention to you. So, I will sit on it for three months. And then we will share it out. But for God's sake, be careful don't go flash with the cash as this will draw attention to you, and all this will be for nothing and we'll end up in the nick. You can both trust me, you know where I live – and even if I did a runner, you could soon find me. So, you've got nothing to worry about, trust me." They asked me if they could have a couple of grand each to tide them over. I told them: "Of course, you can, that's fine. I'm not going to tell you boys exactly where these four pubs are, not till the day we do the job but if we work to my plan this will go as sweet as a nut and put a lot of dough in your pocket."

'Michael, weren't you at all nervous?'

'Never been nervous in my life, Bern. Except for hospitals and dying, which is happening now. But I've lived a charmed life and had a bloody good time.'

'No regrets at all, Mike?'

Well, I suppose just a few. I always envied

you and Jean, what you had in life was each other. I suppose I'm an opportunist. I have buggered up so many good relationships, it's not true. But there's no crying over spilt milk. They asked me if I had a good place to stash the cash. "Don't you worry, boys," I said. "It will be as safe as houses, just like being in the Bank of England." Ha ha.

'So where did you put all this money?'

'A place called Thornwood, the other side of Epping, backing onto Epping Forest, down a country lane by the side of the forest. I parked the car, carried the holdall with all the cash and a spade. I chose the spot well; nice and quiet, deep in the forest. I noted exactly where the trees were in relation to where I was going to put the dough. The leaves in the forest were pretty thick so I gently swept them aside and dug a lovely big hole. I had put the holdall into two black bin bags and sealed them well. I filled it in by scattering all the leaves back over it again, then stood well back to look at what I'd done to see if there was any giveaway. Bern, it was perfect.'

'How could you gamble with your life like this, Mike?'

'My life's been one big gamble, Bernard. But I wanted to get all this off my chest and you were the only good friend I could tell it all to. I suppose you're like the father confessor. Don't worry, Bernie, I'll be gone quite shortly; I feel sure of that. And then you can share my secrets. It will be a good story to tell and will surprise a lot of people. Right, let's get back to the story. The week before, I hired a 1960s Ford estate, and I changed the number plates to the ones I already had used before. I told the boys to meet me round my flat on the Saturday night before we pull the job on the Monday. Just to go through things with them to see there was no loose ends. I told them to wear a hat and I gave them a knitted grey balaclava with holes in it. We went through the whole procedure, chapter and verse, like we had rehearsed previously. "He's in there talking for about half an hour always. After twenty minutes we'll get out the car and leave the passenger's door open. Keep your balaclavas rolled up underneath your hat. Don't pull them down till you see him come out the door. I'll get his attention from the front then you can clobber him from behind. I'll cut the chain on his wrist with the bolt cutters and grab the case. You, Jon, get the car keys out of his pocket or if he's got them in his hand. Then get into his car and follow me. Fred and I will be in my car, you follow on behind. Is that clear? No mistakes. This is going to go well. No worries, boys."

'We parked at a distance about half an hour before I knew the guy would arrive. When he pulled up outside the pub, he locked the door and went in. I drove up and parked the estate car in front of his. After a while, the guy came out and we were ready for him. He looked really surprised seeing me in front of him with a balaclava and a pair of bolt croppers. He raised the case in a gesture to hit me with it. Fred whacked him from behind. He went down like a sack of spuds. I cut the chain through the case, put it in the back of my car and got into the driver's seat. Quickly looked back to see if Jon was in the driver's seat of the car behind. I pulled away slowly with Jon following me. I didn't want to bring attention to a fast car get-away. We drove to Camden council estate and parked the car in the garage underneath the flats. Pulling down the door behind us. Jon parked up in the estate within eye distance of the garage to keep a look out. If he saw anybody he was going to hit the horn.

'We turned the headlights on the vehicle so we could see. Low and behold, it was a very good job they had done with the safe deposit box underneath the front seat. Fred doused the box with water. I lit up the torch and burnt the hinges off the box Fred again doused it with water. When I lifted the lid off, we couldn't believe how much cash there was inside, plus what I had in the case. We stashed it all in a large holdall and then put it in two black plastic bin bags. I rang Jon on the phone to see if all was clear before I opened the garage door. He gave me the all-clear. I opened up – door open. Jon drove up with the estate. We quickly put the burning gear in the back. And covered it up with an old blanket. I get into the driver's seat of the estate and pull forward with Jon beside me. Fred went up to the garage in the other car and closed the garage doors. I drove off with Jon, and Fred followed on behind. We drove out to Essex. Parked the dodgy car in an opening to a field that was well concealed by trees. He smothered the inside of the car with petrol, opened the windows and made a fuse. We lit it and drove off quickly. I drove the boys to a nearby tube station, gave them two grand each and said, "Well done, lads, we pulled it off. All we gotta do now is to keep 'shtum'. And then divvy it out in three months' time. I'll get in touch with both of you." With that, they both went into the station. With big grins on their faces.

    'Next thing I had to do was to get rid of the oxyacetylene gear, which I dumped into a river. Then I drove to Thornwood, near Epping Forest, where I hid the cash. We didn't keep in touch at all for those three months – this was my instructions. Three months went by, Bernie, and I hired a car for the day, changed the plates and drove to Thornwood. It was a quiet Sunday morning, nobody around. I parked the car and walked into the forest concealing the spade underneath my jacket. Just in case, but lucky enough, there was nobody around. I found the spot quite easily and proceeded to dig it up. I slipped one bin bag out of the other because the first one was covered in dirt. Filled the hole in, covered it with leaves again and made my way back to the car. I couldn't help feeling very pleased with myself for what had happened – it all went well.

'In those last three months, I had continued life as normal going to the pub at eleven o'clock for my pint. As I normally do. Of course, the conversation in the pub was about the robbery. Lots of fairy tales to what actually happened. But interesting nevertheless. Apparently, the big guy that we clobbered was okay with just a sore head. He carried on coming into the pub on a Monday, but sometimes he would change it to a weekday, but he always came in with another beefy geezer. They certainly learnt their lesson, I suppose. I phoned the boys and told them to meet me round my flat on a Sunday evening. I had bought three beautiful leather cases – one each – also two bottles of Moet & Chandon. For a little drink to celebrate. The boys arrived about six o'clock Sunday evening. "Now lads, I gave you two grand each, but that is a present from me. Not to be taken out of what we are about to divvy up. I picked it all up this morning, so here it is." I opened the bin bag and got the holdall out, unzipped it and tipped it all on the floor. Fred said, "Blimey, I've never seen so much money!" Jon just stood there with his mouth open.

'The landlords of the public houses, when counting their takings, had conveniently put them in packs of £1000 with an elastic band round them, which was most convenient for us. We counted it all out. And then I gave them their 40 per cent, more money than they had anticipated and a lot more than they had ever seen in their life. They were over the moon and so was I. They put their shares in the suitcases and so did I. We then opened the two bottles of champagne, sat back and had a bloody good drink to celebrate. I said, "Now don't be silly, boys, with what do you do with this cash. Don't draw attention to yourself. By all means, buy a nice car just not a Rolls-Royce. Ha ha."

'Jon asked me what I was going to do. I said, "I'm going abroad; I've got some friends living in Spain." Jon said, "Not a bad idea, Mike." Fred added, "That sounds good to me. I love the old current bun and dipping my feet in the sea with all those beautiful girls." We all shook hands and I said, "I don't want to see your ugly faces again, but it has been a pleasure."

'I drove out to the Costa del Sol in my old Mercedes, which now looks bloody marvellous with a new paint job and a reconditioned engine. I really had a soft spot for that old car, Bern, always wanted one. And it went down well with the birds in Spain. Loads of English there, Bernard, some extremely rich, and some dodgy ones with loads of cash. Drinking in the bars every night, I got to know quite a lot of people. One guy I was drinking with in this bar told me he owned it. It was a really good bar but not many people in there. "Would you be interested in selling this?" I asked. "Not the freehold, Mike, but I'll do you a lease, or yearly rental." So, we done a deal. And I took it over a few weeks later. I kept the original stuff, but the trade was not good. Tons of holidaymakers, but not many coming in.

'One evening, two lovely blonde girls came in. They were aged about 20 to 23; really pretty girls with figures that you would die for. I sat down with them and bought them a drink. "Do you own this?" one of them asked. "Yes, I do, darling. Why, would you like a job?" "Really?" came the reply. "Are you offering one?" "I'm offering two for both of you; very good wages, and you keep all your tips, which could be double what I pay you. Plus, free accommodation above the bar. If after some time, you don't like it, I'll pay for your fare back to England." The girls looked at each other, giggled, and said, "We'll think about it and will let you know tomorrow." But tomorrow never came because I slept with both of them that night above the bar. What a night! One of many, as they both accepted the jobs. I had tight white T-shirts with the name of the bar across the front and back. And red hot pants. And high heel shoes. Bern, they looked electric. Both the girls were from Shepherd's Bush in London. Good old cockney girls, streetwise. And plenty of the gift of the gab. They would take the shirt off your back without you realising it had gone. From the first night they started, the trade just went through the ceiling. I was earning well and so were they.'

'What happened, Mike? Why did you leave it all?'

'Well, the bloke I was renting it from could see the business I was doing, and kept upping the ante. And he wasn't the kind of geezer you would fall out with. So, I bowed out and came back home. I kept in touch with the girls, but they left a few months after I did but they both did well. I rented this flat and have been here ever since. I bought a hamburger van and parked it on the industrial site. It used to do well, but I got fed up with it and sold it.

'What did you do with all your money, Mike?'

'I gambled quite a lot, lived the good life and got rid of the bloody lot. The state keeps me now. I have those two ladies you've met, who come in and check on my food and keep the place clean and tidy. They are very kind, Bernie.'

'Is there anything I can do for you, Michael?'

'Not really, Bern, I just go from day to day. The doctors have been very good to me and have told me I haven't long to go, in case I wanted to make arrangements, which I have. I wanted to see you before I pop off to tell you about my life. But it's been good knowing you and Jean. You were both very good friends, always, and I do appreciate that, Bern.'

'Don't be silly, Michael. We both loved you dearly.'

Three days later, I had a phone call from one of the ladies to say that Michael had passed away.

I am now retired living on my own; my dear wife passed away eight years ago. I started to write my autobiography, as requested by my family, the year before she died. I completed it and published it on Amazon. It's called, *Written While I Can Still Remember* and is going quite well. I'm amazed how many people have written to me to tell me that they like it.

So, I decided to write about the wine bar and an episode in my life I did not talk much about; especially what happened four years ago, when Michael asked me to go and see him and told me of his extraordinary life. I thought I would mention it in this book; however, I do not condone in any shape or form the type of life that Michael lived. He was a friend and that was the type of life he wanted to live.

Owning Marsden's Wine Lodge and meeting all the wonderful characters of London was a sheer pleasure for my wife Jean and me. I have no regrets, just happy memories. I hope you all enjoyed this story.

Printed in Great Britain
by Amazon